WORLD WAR II

AFTERMATH OF WORLD WAR II

by Elisabeth Herschbach

FOCUS
READERS®

V⊘YAGER

www.focusreaders.com

Focus Readers is distributed by North Star Editions:
sales@northstareditions.com | 888-417-0195

Produced for Focus Readers by Red Line Editorial.

Content Consultant: Dr. Gideon Mailer, Associate Professor of History, University of Minnesota Duluth

Photographs ©: Shutterstock Images, cover, 1, 8–9, 17, 24–25, 27, 29, 31, 32–33, 35 (Berlin), 35 (surrounding map), 41, 43; Library of Congress, 4–5; AP Images, 7, 14–15, 23; Charles P. Gorry/AP Images, 10; DPA/AP Images, 13; Mitsunori Chigita/AP Images, 18; iStockphoto, 20–21; Henry Burroughs/AP Images, 36; John Zukowsky/Library of Congress, 38–39; Alfred T. Palmer/Farm Security Administration/Office of War Information Color Photographs/Library of Congress, 45

Library of Congress Cataloging-in-Publication Data
Names: Herschbach, Elisabeth, author.
Title: Aftermath of World War II / by Elisabeth Herschbach.
Other titles: Aftermath of World War 2
Description: Lake Elmo, MN : Focus Readers, [2023] | Series: World War II |
   Includes index. | Audience: Grades 4-6
Identifiers: LCCN 2022012755 (print) | LCCN 2022012756 (ebook) | ISBN
   9781637392805 (hardcover) | ISBN 9781637393321 (paperback) | ISBN
   9781637394304 (pdf) | ISBN 9781637393840 (ebook)
Subjects: LCSH: Reconstruction (1939-1951)--Juvenile literature |
   Germany--History--1945-1955--Juvenile literature. |
   Japan--History--Allied occupation, 1945-1952--Juvenile literature. |
   Cold War--Juvenile literature. | World politics--1945-1955--Juvenile
   literature.
Classification: LCC D825 .H3894 2023 (print) | LCC D825 (ebook) | DDC
   940.55--dc23/eng/20220315
LC record available at https://lccn.loc.gov/2022012755
LC ebook record available at https://lccn.loc.gov/2022012756

Printed in the United States of America
Mankato, MN
082022

ABOUT THE AUTHOR

Elisabeth Herschbach is the author of more than 10 books for young readers on a variety of nonfiction topics. She lives in Maryland, where she works as a copy editor.

TABLE OF CONTENTS

CHAPTER 1
A Changed World 5

CHAPTER 2
Occupied Germany and Japan 9

CHAPTER 3
Forming the United Nations 15

CHAPTER 4
The Decline of Empires 21

CHAPTER 5
New Superpowers 25

A CLOSER LOOK
Upheaval in Asia 30

CHAPTER 6
The Berlin Blockade 33

CHAPTER 7
The Cold War 39

A CLOSER LOOK
Social Changes After World War II 44

Focus on the Aftermath of World War II • 46
Glossary • 47
To Learn More • 48
Index • 48

CHAPTER 1

A CHANGED WORLD

In early 1945, the world was fighting a massive war. The **Allied Forces** and the **Axis** powers clashed around the globe. The war in Europe ended on May 8, when Nazi Germany surrendered. But fighting in Asia continued. In early August, the United States dropped two atomic bombs on Japan. The destruction shocked the world. People wondered how much longer the war would last.

US President Harry S. Truman made the decision to drop the atomic bombs on Japan.

On August 14, US President Harry S. Truman called a special press conference. Anxious crowds waited across the street from the White House. Officials and reporters gathered in the president's office. In a calm voice, Truman announced that Japan had agreed to surrender. World War II (1939–1945) was finally over.

Celebrations broke out across the United States and around the world. Crowds paraded in the streets. People waved flags and threw confetti. In New York City, two million people packed into Times Square. Truman's announcement flashed across the Times Tower. The massive crowd cheered for 20 minutes.

Yet the joy and relief were mixed with grief and horror. World War II had been the deadliest conflict in history. More than 60 million people had been killed. Of those, an estimated 40 million

As news of Japan's surrender spread, people held parades in London and cities around the world.

were **civilians**. Many of those civilians died in the **Holocaust**. Nazi Germany had systematically murdered six million Jews. Nazis also killed members of other minority groups. In addition, bombing had destroyed many cities throughout Europe and Asia. Homes and factories lay in ruins.

It would take years to rebuild after the devastation. The effects of the war lasted long after the fighting ended. They also led to great change. In many ways, the world would never be the same.

CHAPTER 2

OCCUPIED GERMANY AND JAPAN

fter the war, the Allied powers faced a difficult task. They wanted to restore peace and stability. They did not want the defeated nations to attack again. However, Germany and Japan needed help rebuilding. Both countries had been badly damaged. Many farms and factories were destroyed during the fighting. Roads and railways had been blown up, too.

Firebombing left several Japanese cities in ruins.

▲ Douglas MacArthur led the Allied occupation of Japan, which lasted from 1945 to 1951.

The Allies decided to **occupy** Germany and Japan. Allied troops would remain in both countries. But instead of fighting, they would act as a military government.

In Japan, the United States took the lead. General Douglas MacArthur was put in charge. He helped set up a new form of government. He also worked to change Japan's **economy**. Before, a few large companies had controlled nearly half of all business in Japan. MacArthur tried to break up this control. He limited Japan's military, too.

Meanwhile, Germany was divided into four zones. The United States, Britain, France, and the Soviet Union each controlled a zone. Together, they worked to keep the Nazis from rising to power again.

One way they did this was by trying Nazis for war crimes. German leader Adolf Hitler had killed himself near the end of the war. So had several other Nazi officials. But the Allies brought surviving Nazi leaders to court. They wanted to hold them accountable for their actions.

The first trial took place in November 1945. It was held in Nuremberg, Germany. When Hitler was in power, this city had been the site of Nazi rallies. These large gatherings built support for the Nazis. Now, the city would be the site of an international military tribunal. Twenty-two of the top Nazi leaders were brought to trial for their role in the Holocaust. Nineteen were convicted. They were charged with war crimes, crimes against peace, and crimes against humanity.

Other Nazi leaders faced trials at later dates or in different locations. Courts were also set up in Asia. There, some Japanese leaders were tried for war crimes. In total, thousands of military and government officials in both Germany and Japan were brought to court.

Critics pointed out flaws in these trials. In both Germany and Japan, many war criminals escaped punishment. In some cases, other people became scapegoats. These less-guilty people were punished while people who had played bigger roles walked free. Critics also pointed out that

At the Nuremberg trials, Nazi leaders were tried by four judges. One judge came from each major Allied power.

Allied forces had committed war crimes, too. But they were never punished.

Nonetheless, the Nuremberg trials were an important milestone. They marked the first time war crimes were brought before an international court. The trials introduced new legal protections for civilians. These protections are still a central part of international law today. The trials also helped expose the extent of the horrors that took place during the Holocaust.

CHAPTER 3

FORMING THE UNITED NATIONS

Another important event that took place after the war was the creation of the United Nations (UN). This international organization was founded in 1945. But plans for it had begun before the war ended.

A similar organization called the League of Nations had been created in 1920. The league was a response to World War I (1914–1918). Its mission was to settle conflicts between countries

The United Nations (UN) was created to help countries work together and solve problems.

before they led to war. However, the league failed at this task. In fact, its weak responses played a role in the start of World War II.

In the fall of 1944, representatives from Britain, China, the United States, and the Soviet Union met to discuss replacing the League of Nations. They wanted to form a new organization that would be more effective.

Leaders chose the name "United Nations" for this new group. This term had been used to describe the Allied countries during the war. Leaders hoped those countries could work together to rebuild the world the war had shattered.

World War II had been truly devastating. In Europe alone, more than 40 million people were uprooted from their homes. Bombed-out cities across Europe and Asia faced food shortages.

▲ Displaced people traveled throughout Europe seeking
shelter. But they were often seen as unwanted outsiders.

Huge numbers of people were hungry and

homeless. Many became sick or died.

Yet world leaders saw reasons for hope. They

thought the UN could help create a better future.

Representatives from 50 countries came together

in April 1945. They worked to draft the UN

charter. This document outlined the UN's main

▲ In 1958, UNICEF and the World Health Organization helped fund hospitals that cared for children in Japan.

goals. One goal was promoting peace and safety. Another was upholding international law. The UN also aimed to improve living conditions around the world. On October 24, 1945, the finished charter was approved.

Over the years, the UN set up many agencies and programs to help carry out its mission. For example, UNICEF was founded in 1946. It brought aid to children who lived in countries damaged by the war. The World Health Organization was set up in 1948. It helped treat and prevent diseases.

The UN also focused on protecting the rights of people around the world. In December 1948, the UN adopted the Universal Declaration of Human Rights (UDHR). This document describes the basic rights that all people should have. These include education and free speech. The UDHR also says people should be free from torture and slavery. The UN said these rights make justice and peace possible. Many countries agreed. Since the UDHR's creation, similar rights have been included in many laws and treaties.

CONSIDER THIS ◀

What rights do you think all people should have? Why?

CHAPTER 4

THE DECLINE OF EMPIRES

When the UN was first founded, it included 51 countries. Over the years, many new nations joined. By 1965, the UN had 117 members. Many were countries that had just gained their independence. Previously, they had been European **colonies**.

Since the 1400s, European countries had been building vast empires. These countries included Britain, France, Spain, and the Netherlands. They

India was a British colony for many years. In 1947, Britain divided it into India and Pakistan, which led to massive migration.

seized and ruled land around the world. However, maintaining overseas colonies was costly. After World War II, many countries had massive war debts. They no longer had as much money or military power.

In addition, Japan had attacked European colonies in Asia and the Pacific. In many cases, Japan drove the Europeans out and took over. As a result, more colonies felt empowered to resist their rulers. Independence movements grew. Some turned violent. Many European nations lacked the resources to fight back. Their empires began to crumble.

By the late 1960s, dozens of British colonies had won their freedom. So did areas ruled by France and the Netherlands. Many new countries formed in Africa, Asia, and the Middle East. After the war ended, many Holocaust survivors had

▲ Barbed wire lines a street in Jerusalem to prevent clashes between Jews and Arabs in 1948.

fled to the Middle East. They settled in Palestine. However, Jewish immigrants often clashed with the Arabs who already lived there. At the time, Palestine was under British control. In 1948, the British left, and the UN divided the land into separate areas for Jews and Arabs. The Jewish area declared independence in May 1948. It became the nation of Israel. War broke out soon after. Arabs and Israelis each fought to control land. Conflict between them continues today.

CHAPTER 5

NEW SUPERPOWERS

As Europe's power declined, two new superpowers emerged. One was the United States. Wartime production had made the United States stronger. Its economy had nearly doubled since the war's start. The United States also had the world's largest navy and air force.

The Soviet Union had also gained power. During the war, Soviet forces drove German troops out of Eastern Europe. They fought in

The United States built thousands of ships and airplanes during World War II.

Estonia, Latvia, Lithuania, and part of Finland. After the war, the Soviet Union took over these areas.

Other countries in Eastern Europe became satellite states. Officially, they were separate countries. But their governments had close ties to the Soviet Union. These countries included Bulgaria, Czechoslovakia, Hungary, Poland, and Romania. Albania and Yugoslavia were also satellite states for a time.

The United States and the Soviet Union did not trust one another. Each saw the other's growing influence as a threat. The two powers had opposing economic and political systems. The United States was based on capitalism and democracy. In a capitalist system, businesses are privately owned. In a democracy, people vote for their leaders. In contrast, the Soviet Union was based on Communism, and it had a single-party state. In Communism, the government controls all businesses and industries. Often, only one political party is allowed.

SOVIET EXPANSION

Finland

Estonia

Latvia

Lithuania

East Germany

Poland

Czechoslovakia

Hungary

Romania

Yugoslavia

Bulgaria

Albania

Soviet Union

N
W E
S

◼ Soviet Union in 1938
◼ Land gained after World War II
◻ Satellite states

As the Soviet Union expanded, Communism spread throughout Eastern Europe. President Truman worried that it would start spreading in Western Europe, too. If more countries became Communist, capitalist countries like the United States would have less global power.

So, Truman created a plan. He knew countries in Western Europe needed help to rebuild after the war. The United States often tried to stay out of European politics. However, Truman decided to help the war-torn countries recover. Otherwise, they might turn to the Soviet Union instead.

In March 1947, Truman gave a speech. He said the United States would help any country facing a Communist takeover. The United States would give countries money and military support. This pledge became known as the Truman Doctrine. It became a key part of US foreign policy.

By December 1949, the United States had sent one million tons (0.9 million metric tons) of food to Greece.

Truman later signed the Marshall Plan. This plan sent aid to European nations. It gave out more than $13 billion. The funds were used to rebuild cities, roads, and factories. This aid helped European economies grow. It was useful for US trade, too. A stable Europe could buy more goods from the United States.

The Marshall Plan helped Europe recover. It reinforced the United States' role as a global superpower. It also fed the growing tensions between the United States and the Soviet Union.

UPHEAVAL IN ASIA

World War II brought great changes to Asia as well. In Japan, US General Douglas MacArthur worked to create a new **constitution** for the country. Military leaders could not be part of the new government. And Japan's armed forces could be used only for defense.

The occupation of Japan ended in 1952. By then, Japan's government and economy had become stable. But Japan had lost much of its empire. After losing World War II, Japan gave up the territories it had acquired in East Asia and the western Pacific. These included colonies in China, Taiwan, and Korea. Conflicts broke out in many of these areas.

In China, the Chinese Communist Party clashed with the Nationalist Party. A bloody civil war broke out. The Communists won in 1949. As a result, the Nationalists fled to the island of

🔺 US forces helped South Korean soldiers fight back when North Korea invaded.

Taiwan. They set up a government there. Mainland China became a Communist country.

Korea also faced postwar conflict. The United States and the Soviet Union divided Korea into two occupation zones. The Soviets installed a Communist government in North Korea. The United States set up a military government in South Korea. The two superpowers withdrew in 1948 and 1949. Then, North Korea invaded South Korea in 1950. A war raged for three years. Fighting stopped in 1953. But Korea remains divided today.

CHAPTER 6

THE BERLIN BLOCKADE

The Soviet Union and the United States also disagreed over plans for postwar Germany. By 1948, the United States, Britain, and France wanted Germany to become an independent nation again. For that to happen, the four occupation zones had to join back together. Germany's economy also needed help. Soviet leader Joseph Stalin disagreed. The Soviets had suffered great losses while fighting Germany.

World War II destroyed many cities and towns throughout Germany.

If Germany reunited and recovered, it could become a threat to the Soviet Union again. Stalin wanted to keep Germany weak and divided. He also wanted to keep control of German factories and industries. They had been producing money and supplies for the Soviet Union. So, Stalin wanted the eastern part of Germany to remain under Soviet control.

US, British, and French leaders decided to act without Stalin. They merged their three zones. The combined zones now formed a single area in western Germany. The United States offered Marshall Plan assistance to Germany. The Allies also introduced a new form of money. Germany's old currency had become almost worthless. The new currency helped Germans buy more things. But the Soviet zone still had the old, worthless money.

Stalin was enraged. He saw these actions as a threat to his interests. So, in June 1948, he ordered a blockade of Berlin. This city was

OCCUPIED GERMANY

Berlin

British occupation zone

Soviet occupation zone

Saar Protectorate

American occupation zone

French occupation zone

▲ US and British pilots made a total of 277,000 flights during the Berlin airlift.

Germany's capital. And it was in eastern Germany. That part of the country was under Soviet control. However, like the rest of Germany, Berlin was divided into four zones. The Soviets controlled East Berlin. The United States, Britain, and France controlled the western part of the city.

During the blockade, Stalin cut off all land access to West Berlin. No supplies could get in by road, rail, or canal. Some 2.5 million people were trapped. Stalin hoped to force West Berlin to surrender. Then it would merge with the surrounding Soviet zone. But the United States and its allies organized an airlift. Planes dropped food, medicine, fuel, and other essentials into West Berlin. The airlift continued for 11 months. Allied pilots dropped more than 2 million tons (1.8 million metric tons) of supplies.

The Soviets lifted the Berlin blockade in May 1949. However, the city stayed divided. So did the rest of Germany. Tensions between the United States and the Soviet Union also increased. This tension soon became a fierce power struggle known as the Cold War.

CONSIDER THIS ◀

Do you think countries should give aid to former enemies after a war? Why or why not?

CHAPTER 7

THE COLD WAR

Soon after the Berlin blockade, Germany split into two separate nations. One was West Germany. This area had been occupied by the United States, Britain, and France. Now, it had a democratic government. Its economy was capitalist. The Soviet zone became East Germany. Its government was Communist.

West and East Germany would remain separate for the next 45 years. This division was mirrored

A wall separated Soviet-controlled East Berlin from the rest of the city.

in Europe as a whole. Western and Eastern Europe split into opposing sides. The countries of Western Europe sided with the United States. In 1949, they formed a military alliance called the North Atlantic Treaty Organization (NATO). Members promised to defend one another from Soviet attacks. In 1955, the Communist countries of Eastern Europe formed their own defense alliance with the Soviet Union. It was called the Warsaw Pact.

Each side tried to gain more power than the other. This competition soon took a dangerous turn. The United States had made the world's first atomic bombs. It dropped two on Japan in August 1945. The Soviet Union had also been working on developing nuclear weapons. Four years later, it succeeded. The Soviet Union tested its first atomic bomb in August 1949. This set off an arms

The Soviets had developed S-125 missiles by the 1960s. These nuclear missiles were designed to shoot at aircraft.

race between the two superpowers. Both sides raced to stockpile nuclear weapons. They also competed to build bigger, stronger bombs. Some of the weapons they developed were 1,000 times more powerful than the bombs dropped on Japan. And they could be launched from thousands of miles away.

However, these powerful weapons were not used to attack. The stakes were too high. If one country attacked with its nuclear weapons, the other would retaliate. Both countries would be destroyed. So would much of the rest of the world. For this reason, the two superpowers never fought each other with nuclear weapons.

The superpowers did get involved in other conflicts, though. Wars in Korea and Vietnam were two examples. The United States and the Soviet Union backed opposite sides in these wars. Each superpower tried to help its side win. However, their actions actually made the conflicts worse. Foreign support made the wars last longer. More people died as a result.

Space exploration became another way to show dominance. Both superpowers wanted to send a spaceship to the moon. They also raced to set

ЧЕЛОВЕК В КОСМОСЕ!
КАПИТАН ПЕРВОГО ЗВЕЗДОЛЕТА—НАШ, СОВЕТСКИЙ!

Великая победа
разума и труда
МИР РУКОПЛЕЩЕТ
ЮРИЮ ГАГАРИНУ

ПРОЛЕТАРИИ ВСЕХ СТРАН,
СОЕДИНЯЙТЕСЬ!

Орган
Центрального
Комитета
ВЛКСМ

КОМСОМОЛЬСКАЯ
ПРАВДА

Год издания 36-й
№ 88 (11028)   Четверг, 13 апреля 1961 г.   Цена 2 коп.

К Коммунистической партии и народам

▲ On April 12, 1961, Yuri Gagarin made headlines by
becoming the first person in space.

records along the way. Soviet scientists launched
the first spacecraft. They also sent the first
human into space. But US astronauts first landed
on the moon.

The power struggle between the United States
and the Soviet Union lasted for decades. Finally,
the Soviet Union collapsed in 1991. The Cold War
was over. But it had brought sweeping changes to
the world, just as World War II had done.

SOCIAL CHANGES AFTER WORLD WAR II

World War II changed many areas of life. During the war, doctors created new medicines. They found better ways to do **blood transfusions** and surgeries. These changes helped people around the world receive better health care.

Wartime research also led to new technology. Scientists learned ways to use radar and microwaves. Computers improved. And military rockets were adapted for space exploration.

In many countries, the war brought women new opportunities. While men were off fighting battles, more women entered the workforce. They took jobs to help with the war effort. After the war, some women went back to more traditional roles at home. But attitudes about gender roles

Black soldiers and workers played a crucial role in the US war effort. They also helped call for equal rights.

had begun to shift. This change paved the way for greater equality for women.

World War II also played an important role in the civil rights movement in the United States. Large numbers of Black Americans joined the US military. They risked their lives to fight for their country. Many earned honors for their courage and skill. Yet in the military and back home, Black Americans still faced **discrimination**. Activists drew more people's attention to these problems. This awareness helped fuel efforts for equal rights.

THE AFTERMATH OF WORLD WAR II

Write your answers on a separate piece of paper.

1. Write a paragraph summarizing the key ideas of Chapter 6.

2. Do you think international organizations like the United Nations can prevent wars? Back up your answer with reasons.

3. When did the occupation of Japan end?

   A. 1945
   B. 1952
   C. 1991

4. If one member of the Warsaw Pact was attacked, what would happen?

   A. NATO members would come to its defense.
   B. Other members of the Warsaw Pact would attack it, too.
   C. Other members of the Warsaw Pact would fight to defend it.

Answer key on page 48.

GLOSSARY

Allied Forces
The victorious countries of World War II, including Britain, France, the Soviet Union, and the United States.

Axis
The side of World War II that included Germany, Italy, Japan, and their allies.

blood transfusions
Treatments in which blood is added to the body of a person who is sick or hurt.

civilians
People who are not in the military.

colonies
Areas controlled by a country that is far away.

constitution
A document laying out the basic beliefs and laws of a nation or state.

discrimination
Unfair treatment of a person or group based on race, gender, or other factors.

economy
The system of goods, services, money, and jobs in a certain place.

Holocaust
The murder of millions of Jews and others by the Nazis during World War II.

occupy
To control an area using military power.

TO LEARN MORE

BOOKS

Hudak, Heather C. *Nuclear Weapons and the Arms Race.* New York: Crabtree Publishing, 2018.

Medina, Nico. *What Was the Berlin Wall?* New York: Penguin Workshop, 2019.

Otfinoski, Steven. *The Cold War.* New York: Scholastic, 2018.

NOTE TO EDUCATORS

Visit **www.focusreaders.com** to find lesson plans, activities, links, and other resources related to this title.

INDEX

Berlin blockade, 35–37, 39

China, 16, 30–31
colonies, 21–22, 30
Communism, 27–28, 30–31, 39–40

Eastern Europe, 25–26, 28, 40

Israel, 22–23

Korea, 30–31, 42

MacArthur, Douglas, 10–11, 30
Marshall Plan, 29, 34

North Atlantic Treaty Organization (NATO), 40
nuclear weapons, 40–42
Nuremberg trials, 11–13

occupied Germany, 10–11, 33–37, 39

occupied Japan, 10–11, 30

Truman, Harry S., 6, 28–29

United Nations (UN), 15–19, 21, 23

Vietnam, 42

Warsaw Pact, 40
Western Europe, 28, 40

Answer Key: **1.** Answers will vary; **2.** Answers will vary; **3.** B; **4.** C